TRUCKING COMPANY

How to become a true professional
brokerage and freight forwarder.
The complete guide to starting your
own trucking business

VINCENT STIVENS

TABLE OF CONTENTS

INTRODUCTION

The trucking company, freight liner, is a trucking company that services in the united states, southern California. It also services in other countries like Mexico and Canada. The Freightliner is a trucking company specializing in hauling freight or transporting goods from one place to another.

The Freightliner was founded by two friends who are named Jim Jan nard and Tim Skelly. They begin their business by going door to door, asking for people's business. They would then buy the trucks from leasing companies, so they call themselves Freightliner leasing corps (FLLC). After purchasing a car from good companies, they would hire drivers with their own money and pay them with their own money. And at first, they were having a hard time getting customers, so they would put signs on the highway and in front of stores and other places that would get people's attention.

The Freightliner has been around for a while. The company started as Freightliner crop then changed to freight liner corp. The company is well known for trucking because it offers the lowest price than any other trucking company that does the same thing as hauling freight. Freight liner is known for delivering all over the united states, Canada and Mexico. They offer free moving to cover areas in California, Nevada, Arizona, or Texas with no extra cost for traveling more than

300 miles from their headquarters in southern California or atlas terminal in El Paso, Texas. But some fees could occur to charge for traveling more than 400 miles from their offices or airport located in El Paso, Texas, than 300 miles from their headquarters. This fee is charged per 25-mile increments, which starts at 6 dollars per quarter of a mile. The company also offers its customers a free 10,000-mile warranty for its trucks. The Freightliner provides the lowest price that any of the other trucking companies offer, except the ones that are state-run trucks. The company has only one location where it operates out of its airports in Las Vegas or southern California. And they stay there because the laws are more favorable there than in other states or countries. The Freightliner has become known as a handy place to get some work and support your family off hauling freight. And how relaxed it is for them to hire people out there for moving their stuff from one place to another and everything else that they need to be done on their properties from residential houses, apartments buildings, and commercial buildings. And because of the location they are in, it is easy to keep employees and not have to burden about whether or not you will be able to get your freight where you need it to. It is also an excellent place for you to be able to save on the cost of fuel. Many people had said the cost of energy that when they compared the fuel price with other companies that do the same job as them, they didn't think they could profit from transporting freight at such a low cost.

START-UP BUSINESS

B usiness is like war. It requires thorough preparation and strategy before getting into it. Going in blind can obliterate your business in no time. Hence, this part details the costs associated with starting a trucking business and how to determine the profitability of your enterprise. Most importantly, this part includes a plan that you can use as a roadmap to begin your trucking company on the right footing and increase your chances of survival.

What to Expect When Running a Trucking Business

There is no secret that owning and running a trucking business successfully is hard work. You'll likely spend a big chunk of your time (if you are an owner-operator) hauling for your customers. Add to this the other duties small business operators have to perform, such as finding customers and building relationships, and you have a demanding task ahead of you. All these tasks require your time. This means that you may have to spend more time away from home, especially in the beginning, while putting the various business systems together.

Safety Rules and Regulations

Compliance with safety rules and regulations is essential in the trucking industry. There are plenty of these rules and regulations, which I'll discuss in more detail later in the book. Some of them include the following:

- Canadian Safety Association (C.S.A.) safety standards (where applicable).
- The allowable hours of work for your drivers.
- Physical qualifications for truck drivers.
- Electronic logging devices for each driver to figure out the weekly hours they have worked.

Don't think of these regulations as a way to punish you. They may even dissuade others from joining the industry and thus improve your prospects of succeeding.

Costs of Starting and Owning a Trucking Company

The amount of money you need to start a trucking company provides different views and answers. This is because startup costs depend on several factors, such as the state that you're in, the size of your fleet, whether you already own a truck and have insurance, and whether you'll haul freight interstate, intrastate, or both.

Typically, a small trucking company costs about $25,000 to $40,000 to get started. This figure excludes the costs of purchasing equipment. Here are the significant expenses you'll pay during the truck business startup phase:

- Insurance down payment of between $2,000 and $4,800 a truck annually.
- The price of a truck. Which varies from $15,000 to $175,000 depending on its condition, type, and age or if you choose to buy one outright.
- The state-specific tax of about $500 a truck.
- International Registration Plan (IRP) costs between $500 and $3,000.
- Business registration cost of $50 to $300, depending on your state.
- USDOT (Motor Carrier) number costs from $300 to $499.
- The International Fuel Tax Agreement (IFTA) report costs around $150.
- Unified Carrier Registration (U.C.R.) of $69 and above.
- Trucking insurance ranging from $9,000 to $12,000 a truck annually.

I am appointing a Blanket of Coverage (BOC-3) processing agent costs from $10 to $50.

Adding up all the expenses listed above means that you'll need to set aside from $28,000 to $200,000. Note that this is an estimate. You still need to work out the exact amounts of each expense necessary to start your company. Also, you need to factor in other costs, such as meals, salaries, bookkeeping, parking, and tolls.

Why You Should Start with One Truck

Nothing beats growing a business organically. What do I mean by this? You see, you can choose to buy six trucks at the start of your business. If you start such a trucking business from scratch with no knowledge, skills, and experience, then the mistakes you're bound to make can wipe out the company in no time. This happens because you would have tried to jump the growth steps necessary to build the right competencies. And without the required fundamental skills, the chances of succeeding diminish greatly.

It is like these people who win the lottery and wind up broke within a few years. The lottery windfall finds them with no money management skills and all the bad habits of living. Most of them, inevitably, focus on consumption and soon use up all the money. They, essentially, return to the level where they were before winning the lottery. Money, like all tools, is an accelerator. And you can only safely accelerate something that's built on a sound foundation.

Starting with one truck provides ample opportunities to learn safely while making money. Here are some advantages to this approach:

- You reduce the amount of startup capital to a manageable level. This minimizes the stress of looking for funding, which is better for you and your family.
- You minimize the risk of business loss. One truck means less complexity. And the simpler the

business, the easier it is to run and to correct mistakes quickly. Big companies cannot respond swiftly when changes need to be made. But you will if you're operating with a single truck.

- Most importantly, you give yourself the time to build systems to run your business more efficiently in the future. Think about this for a moment. Would it be easier to make a safety system for one truck or a fleet often? Of course, it would be easier to do so if you run one truck. And when you add a second truck, all you do is duplicate what you would have already done. This means that you'll grow your business quickly as time progresses.

The systems to consider building while operating one truck include human resources, information technology, marketing, sales, operations, technology, etc. The power of a system is that it frees resources and enables you to do more with less. For example, with a design, you can onboard a new driver much faster than another business and make fewer mistakes. Furthermore, systems allow you to deliver consistent performance, which is key to building a reputation that is so necessary for the trucking industry.

What Profits Can I Make in a Trucking Business?

The profitability of your trucking business, like in any industry, depends mostly on how well you run your company. Well-planned trucking businesses manage cash flow and avoid deadhead miles average around 7% of gross income per year in profit. This means that, for a company generating $300,000 of annual revenue per truck, it will profit $21,000 from every Truck.

The timing of getting paid after doing the work affects your business profitability. Late payments may push you to begin shortcutting important work like truck maintenance or borrow a lot more. If you don't do maintenance in time, your trucks may often break down and cost you more in repairs. The repair costs will eat away your profits. Borrowing money isn't free. It costs money and can pull your business back instead of strengthening it.

Furthermore, as a startup, keep in mind that it may take several months before your company turns a sizable profit. This reason, and the one above, provide convincing evidence why having three to six months of emergency cash is vital for your business. It will help you weather the storm if you meet unforeseen events and circumstances.

You're probably wondering how much money you'll personally make when running your own trucking company. Well, this depends on your skills, experience, and competency. If you are good at getting customers and delivering what you promise, you'll make more money than the average small carrier. Trucking business owners with more experience can make around $100,000 or more, while the less-experienced earn about $35,000 per year. Most owners make a healthy $50,000 annually.

Make sure that you have your truck, buy truck insurance, maintenance, and fuel. So, you do a lot more work than a driver working for a large carrier. However, your focus is not just to make money but to build an asset that will deliver cash flow even when you're no longer actively working. This can only happen if you create effective systems to run your business.

How to Estimate the Revenue of Your Trucking Company

It is essential before you start your trucking company to know what revenue to expect. You're fortunate because the way to figure out your potential income is already available. And I'll show you here how to do it painlessly. There is no standard revenue per mile general in the industry. So, you have to figure out your numbers. Here's how to do it.

- Select the Industry to Support

Your first task is to choose the industry in which you want to operate. This is important, as you'll see below when selecting a freight lane. More importantly, doing this enables you to buy the right truck. Imagine purchasing a reefer and choosing projects that require a flatbed. That would be catastrophic, isn't it?

So, choosing the industry precedes the purchasing of equipment. For example, if you choose to serve the fresh produce industry, you'll need to buy a reefer. Furthermore, selecting the industry helps you to learn the specifics like seasonality and price variations. This, in turn, allows you to plan your business much better than without this knowledge and information.

- Choose Freight Lane to Work

A freight lane called a carrier lane or shipping lane is a route that you routinely run to deliver truckloads. It runs from point A to point B. For example, it could run from New York to Los Angeles.

Now, it's vital to select a shipping lane that services your chosen industry and is closer to where you live. The latter is essential because you'll be able to maximize the time you spend at home. There are

truck drivers that barely see their homes for days or weeks. And this may not be optimal for building healthy family relationships. Ensure that you select carrier lanes that are near transportation "hot markets." Why is this important? Because it is easier to find loads where the demand is high. Markets like Chicago, Atlanta, Memphis, Texas, Louisiana, Seattle, and California are busy trucking companies.

- Figure Out the Pay-Per-Mile on Your Carrier Lane

These limited guidelines below will teach you how to determine pay-per-mile on your carrier lane and reveal your shapeliness profitability. Let's go over the six steps.

The first thing to do is go to a free trucking load board and look for freight in your shipping lane. A load board is nothing but an online system that lets shippers and freight brokers broadcast their freight loads.

Second, get prices per mile on a minimum of 10 truckloads. The more, the better because the accuracy of your figures will improve.

Thirdly, add the prices of each of the ten loads and their corresponding miles. Now divide the total

of the prices by the total number of miles. The number you have computed is the average price

of each load per mile of the lane.

Alternatively, compute each load's pay-per-mile by dividing the price by the total number of miles of each shipment. Then, add all the pay-per-mile numbers and divide the final answer by 10. That gives you the average price per mile of your selected freight lane in one direction.

Trucking/Freight Broker Job and Responsibilities

Trucking brokers can be viewed as the transportation and logistics industry's matchmakers.

They work to match a shipper with a carrier to get cargo from Point A to Point B. Determining a freight broker's roles and responsibilities will help you assess your work readiness.

5 Things to Do as a Trucking Broker

1. Shippers and carriers to get a fair rate for a specific load and making
2. Monitor the shipment movement by keeping in contact with drivers and shippers.
3. If necessary, make arrangements for load storage.
4. You are troubleshooting any problems that happen during load movement.
5. Confirm with truckers and consignees that a load is delivered on time and according to load information.

To do this, you need a few essential skills and mindset. Let's look at those for a moment.

11 Essential Skills of a Trucking Broker

If you plan to become a trucking broker, you need to have a few specific characteristics to have a better chance at success. This doesn't mean you can't become a trucking broker without these traits; it just means developing these traits or compensating in other areas. Let's discuss these ten very essential and essential skills a trucking broker should have.

Education and Training

Of course, you need to continually learn and improve your education and skill level, new employee about a freight load or a savvy trucking company about a lower freight rate. You need the skills to convey your message effectively.

A trucking broker will be more successful if they like what they are doing and are driven by passion. More resources for a hobby, or anything else that causes your enthusiasm to work as a trucking/freight broker, motivation is key to getting through the day. Interestingly enough, money isn't the top reason for most freight brokers.

As you can tell, a typical trucking broker's daily routine involves a lot of details. If you deal with this too long, it is easy to lose sight of the big picture. Don't lose your focus and start settling for short-term advantages rather than long-term benefits.

This is when your business will lose competitive advantage and stop improving. A strategic mindset causes you to continually evaluate and refine how you run your business and keeps you learning new things.

These are also the individuals who are aware of what's currently going on in the industry, especially when it comes to competitors and partners, so a business can quickly adapt to any negative market changes.

Successful trucking brokers need to set goals and use them to define tactical actions that gain the results they want. The preparations for a new business and the details involved.

However, a lot of time, success comes down to hitting the ground running even if you don't have everything ready to go yet. As long as you are doing something tangible, you can keep refining and redefining as you go.

This is why setting benchmarks and milestones will help you to have success as a freight broker. We'll discuss this more in-depth at a later point in this book.

The very culture of trucking brokering is customer-oriented. A happy customer will come back and become a loyal customer. Successful brokers know they need to be helpful and devoted to a customer's interest to keep the business profiting.

Focus on speedy and safe delivery for shipments and on time, decent pay for carriers. When you have a deep base of repeat customers, you can be very responsive and anticipatory of their needs.

Having an attitude of "what can I do to help?" will keep your business viable.

As cargo moves from shipper to consignee, several things are happening at once. And just as many things can go wrong too. You need to anticipate these problems and have various response mechanisms to address anything that can go wrong.

A truck breaks down, or a major accident occurs. You need more than just a Plan B in place; you need to have multiple backup options.

It is crucial to have the big picture in mind and even keep future events in mind. However, this doesn't mean you should lose sight of the details.

The most important thing is to know what to do first. When you see the difference between necessary, urgent, or essential, you will reduce your decision-making time in half.

Knowing how to prioritize tasks is a must as a trucking broker. And it's just as vital that you know how to do things quickly.

You can't grow a successful trucking brokerage business if you don't build and develop a relationship for the long term. During every engagement, you need to cooperate with various individuals and organizations with multiple cultures and values.

You have a helpful and beneficial relationship that can grow over time. Remember the trust you earn over time from your customers is the biggest asset you will have own in this business

In our case, that is likely to be a better freight rate) through negotiation, then you will not only win their business but a meaningful, long-lasting relationship as well.

One essential part of being a successful trucking and freight broker is communicating with your customers.

You can give the right answer at the wrong time and lose a deal. Remember, in the freight industry, and communication is everything. Even when freight is missing, always communicate with the shipper and receiver, keep them informed.

Let them know that their freight is your biggest priority, and you will do everything in your power to make sure the goods arrive in good condition and on time.

Lastly, a freight broker needs always to know what is going on in the fast-paced environment around them while performing various tasks.

Most people think they can multi-task, but it is another thing to master. To multi-task smartly, you need to focus on your strengths and not your weaknesses.

10 Steps to Becoming a Successful Trucking Broker

1. Get Proper education/training
2. Name your business
3. Incorporate your business
4. Have a Business Plan
5. Gather up enough money to get started
6. Get all required licenses
7. Obtain Proper Bond and Insurance
8. Set up your office/home office
9. Finding Clients
10. Ongoing Marketing

Training Requirements to Become A Trucking Broker

Many schools offer training courses and various degrees, such as supply chain management, but these are not educational requirements. As far as schooling goes, all that is needed is a Diploma

Training

The easiest way to be trained is by having an entry-level your feet wet. But I can also understand that such jobs are not readily available to

You'll also gain essential practical knowledge and hands-on learning.

There are many on and offline schools; it is hard for me to list them all here in this book. But you can do a simple Google search on "Freight Broker Training Schools Near me" and see a list of great names in the result.

There are many online schools, but I would hate to mention any names as I have not personally tried their courses.

But as I said, a simple Google search will reveal all the details, and then you can contact them one by one and compare the cost along with the length of their training classes.

Let's consider how you can set up goals and achieve them for success.

SERVICE BUSINESS ANALYSIS

Market Description of the Trucking Industry:

The trucking industry (also denoted to as the logistics or transportation industry) includes the carriage and delivery of industrial and commercial goods by means of commercial motor vehicles (CMV).

The trucking industry offers a vital service to the American economy by moving large amounts of raw supplies, works in course, and complete goods over land, naturally from industrial plants to retail dispersal centers. Trucks in America are responsible for most freight movement over land and are important tools in the transportation, manufacturing, and warehousing industries.

It is primarily engaged in furnishing "over-the-road" trucking services; they have improved to the current changes in market situations and the decelerating economy by picking to benefit both the -than-truckload;(LTL) and the truckload;(T.L.)

The sector, to capitalize on growth opportunities and increase company revenue.

The trucking industry exists in a competitive market that experience uncertainty, particularly during a low economy, the rising cost of fuel, maintenance, insurance, and taxes.

Advances in current technology have allowed noteworthy improvements in the trucking industry. Trucks are usually prepared automatic transmissions and with satellite communication features are acquiring popularity; truck stops including internet access and hospitality services are now commonplace.

The technology was necessary for proper communication, route guidance, and road conditions.

Our trucks are also in compliance with the U.S. Environmental Protection Agency (E.P.A.) requirements.

Competition and Buying Patterns

Although there are significant players in the marketable carrier market units, the market keeps to be highly fragmented. Rendering to on-line data research, there are twelve freight and commercial companies in Buckhannon, West Virginia. They offer a variety of trucking facilities, delivery only, smaller freights under 100 pounds to hauling more enormous truckloads locally and across the country.

Market research shows that companies who manufacture products of a more considerable proportion value on-time deliveries, remarkable handling capabilities, and less-than-truckload; (LTL) orders. These companies are also pricing sensitive. Customer referrals and the carrier's reputation are believed to be a strong influence in buying services.

Frequently word of mouth marketing provides more business than advertising. However, advertising in certain areas (such as trade journals) creates awareness of its existence, skill level, premium service, and reputation. The industry is geographically oriented; most of the clients are in Buckhannon, West Virginia; though, by getting on accounts with customers in other states, has the opportunity to increase revenue, expand their services, and, decrease operating costs; scheduling a delivery and pickup in or close the drivers last delivery last stop decreases the company overhead of a truck returning to Buckhannon with an unfilled trailer.

Web Plan Summary

Currently does not have a website. An internet site will be a thought for the future, offering available services of scheduling a delivery, current information on the trucking industry, and for the client to check the delivery status of a recent shipment.

Website Marketing Strategy

The upcoming website will be endorsed on company trucks, advertising materials, invoices And other business materials. Links to other websites that pertain to the trucking industry, such as the American Trucking Association website and other portals worldwide, will be beneficial.

Development Requirements

A professional company website would be developed, perhaps with experience and knowledge in the trucking industry's logistics. Pre-packaged solutions with numerous companies and Web hosting resources will also be considered.

Strategy and Implementation Summary

- Emphasize service – will distinguish them by providing premium services to their clients. They will establish a new business by offering competitive prices and flexibility for our clients' needs.
- Build a relationship-oriented business – Establishing long-term relationships with customers is a vital attribute. Their clients give them their trust and confidence that they will provide them the delivery services they require.
- Focus on target markets - needs to focus their offerings to the manufacturing plants in Buckhannon and other regions of the U.S. They do not want to compete with other trucking services that deliver only locally and want to sell their services to other manufacturers across the country, not just those in their local area of Buckhannon, West Virginia.

SWOT Analysis

There has a valuable inventory of strengths that has contributed

To the success of the company since 1983. These strengths comprise knowledgeable and experienced staff with a strong vision of the trucking industry, excellent client services, and market needs,

They are flexible concerning the client's delivery needs and will go wherever they need them to go; whether they have a full-load; (F.L.) or less-than-full-load; (LTL) or need rush delivery, they get the job done efficiently and on time and, their prices beat those of their competitors.

It is an icon in the town of Buckhannon; they have built an excellent reputation with their clients, in the community and, in the trucking industry.

Strengths are a valued asset for a fruitful business, and it is also essential to know the weaknesses then deal with them. These weaknesses are the dependence on economic conditions. The effect that the economy has on the general public also affects clients; if their business decreases, the trucking industry also suffers.

The greatest weakness at present is their trucks; they have over 1,000,000 miles on them. They need new trucks with better fuel efficiency to keep up with the industry's demands and E.T.A. requirements. The new trucks will expand their services, creating more business revenue to pay debts and generate more business during the low economy.

The biggest threat to and the overall industry, just like their weakness, is the uncertainty of current economic conditions and their dependency on the economy to create the business. When the economy is frail and weak, it distresses

The manufacturers; depend on the manufacturers for business just as the manufacturers rely on their clients, retailers, construction companies, and the general consumers who purchase their products.

Strengths

The staff is experienced and knowledgeable in the trucking industry's logistics; they are courteous and provide excellent services to all clients. Strong relationships with clients, offering flexible arrangements for rush deliveries. Competitive prices provide repeat and referral business. Long term contracts with major manufacturing companies in Buckhannon. Premium quality service and on-time delivery.

Weaknesses

- The business has been unpredictable throughout the vagueness of economic conditions.
- The needs new trucks. These trucks will offer better emissions control, better fuel efficiency, and lessen our cost of overhead to keep. These new

trucks will permit us to increase our services, generating more revenue to pay our Debts.

Opportunities

They are increasing sales opportunities beyond the "100-mile" targeted area. Current clients with manufacturing plants in other cities and states. Strategic alliances offering resources for referrals and marketing to extend reach to potential new clients.

Threats

The economy's downturn has impacted sales in the first quarter of 2010—the rising cost of fuel, maintenance, and repairs. The winter weather in West Virginia during December, January, and February can be a safety hazard; getting around the mountains to the main highway can difficult and dangerous for 18-wheeler trucks.

Competitive Edge

It will succeed in establishing a competitive edge, contacting more companies in their targeted market, increase its level of customer contacts, and provide services that its competitors seem to lack.

Additionally, It possesses all the necessary skills and drivers available to provide the clients' services.

The expansion of services will strengthen their business, promote word of mouth marketing and networking, and create more business.

Marketing Strategy

It has positioned itself as an icon in Buckhannon. Their clients are provided with high-quality services at a very competitive price.

SETTING UP YOUR BUSINESS PLAN

Now that you know how to start your trucking business, this part will give you knowledge on drawing a business plan and its essentials, including creating a mission and vision statement, conducting competitor analysis, and calculating the cost of starting a trucking company, among other things.

A trucking company, just like any other business, requires a business plan, which is the mirror of the business. It's a clear reflection of the business, which is not only useful for personal purposes, but it's vital for seeking prospective partners, investors, or financial assistance from banks.

Your business plan should contain a clear mapped out list of what the company does, its competitors, future predictions of its financial position, and how you plan to achieve the goals you have set out for yourself.

Remember that a business plan is a continuous process that requires you to appraise and update it regularly to ensure that you meet your goals. It's also important to note that every business plan is unique, and to this effect, yours should stand out.

The following outlines the key elements in a trucking company business plan:

This is an introduction to your company and what it hopes to achieve in the future. It should cover a maximum of two pages and a minimum of one page. It should be clear, concise, and attractive to the reader. It should outline the company's objectives and how they will be met. This should also feature its mission, services, financial information, performance, and intended plans. This is also known as the company's profile.

This part gives an overall description of your company's vision and mission and why it's unique compared to its competitors. It should have information on the founder, why it was started, the year it was created, the business location, and the specific goods you intend to haul. As your company grows, this is where you will include the organization structure. It's important to know that a vision statement is different from a mission statement.

A mission statement clearly outlines what your company does, why it does it, and the benefits of what it does. It shows what your company aims to achieve and the path it will take in the future. It makes your company stand out from its competitors, and it outlines the common goal that your company and future employees need to achieve. It should be an eloquent and memorable sentence.

a) Define your purpose

This should answer questions like why does your company exist? Who does it aim to serve? How will you deliver the service, and why is your service valuable? Think of the benefits in terms of impact on the community, employees, shareholders, or customers.

b) Be particular

This simply means avoid any jargon. It should be easy to remember to communicate well with the intended members, for example, employees. The terms are understandable and relevant to your business.

c) Inspire

Make it dynamic and inspirational to encourage your employees to work hard towards the company's vision.

d) Be brief

While large companies have a lengthy mission statement, making it short and concise is the ideal way of remembering your company's core values, which will guide you in the years to come.

Vision Statement

The desired future. It's a description of the end of the business that manages to fulfill its mission. It involves your imagination and dreaming significant about your company. It's meant to inspire your employees to achieve the company's goals.

Your company's brand values should be reflected in your vision statement. Your vision statement should be a reflection of how you want your employees to act and behave. Stop and think about what you want your company to achieve, and don't hold anything back.

Creating A Vision Statement

a) Examine your mission statement

This simply involves writing down what your company does and what purpose it serves. Put it into the present tense.

b) Make it memorable

Dare to dream to make it robust. Ensure that it's to the point and easy to remember. It should answer the questions, what is unique about your services? What will your company be recognized?

c) Shaping your vision formula

Apply this formula:

This formula will help you to identify the accomplishment that you consider to be most important and how to accomplish it within a particular timeline. For instance: will be the top-grossing trucking service provider in the South Coast area by consistently providing reliable and affordable services to farmers.

d) Be committed to the vision

Exert your vision statement in your business planning since it provides your destination. It will help you achieve all of your goals. Ensure you continuously share it with employees and potential partners by printing it out and sticking it to be visible and act as a reminder.

Significant differences between mission statements and vision statements are:

- A mission statement talks about how the business will get to where it wants to be, whereas a vision statement talks about where the company wants to be.
- A mission statement gives answers to the questions, "what do we do? What makes us unique?"
- While a vision statement is based on the future.
- A mission statement addresses both the internal and external members, whereas a vision statement addresses the internal members only.

Services

Clearly outline the goods that your trucking company will haul and the industries that you will work with. Show that your services are essential as they meet the needs demanded by the customer. An example could be transporting fresh produce for farmers to a country where many carriers do not venture.

Market Analysis

This unit should demonstrate how conversant you are with your trucking business in terms of customer needs, what is trending, and why you believe your company can thrive in the already crowded trucking market. The following key points should form the basis of your market analysis:

a) Trucking industry description

You should have excellent knowledge of the trucking industry's size by identifying the major carriers and the biggest shippers.

b) Target market

You should show that your trucking company stands out by specializing in a market that is avoided by large carriers, hence guaranteeing you great returns.

c) Unique characteristics

Identify customer needs that stand out and how your trucking company intends to meet those needs.

d) Size of the primary target market

Have substantial knowledge of your high-ranking market as well as the top customers. For instance, if cattle farmers dominate your area, there is a need to transport the cattle to the slaughterhouse. Knowing the actual number of cattle farmers who are your target market is critical.

e) Market share

This should show how much market your company intends to penetrate within a specific period. The prediction must be reasonable.

f) Pricing and gross margin targets

Clearly outline your trucking company's charging rates and any discounts that may be given. Include your target margin for each service you offer.

g) Competitive analysis

You must know their strengths and weaknesses. Conducting a SWOT analysis is highly recommended.

Swot Analysis

The subject to change if you work on them, for example, reputation and sales. The factors that you have no control over, for example, prices and competitors.

- Strengths – Identify what your trucking company is good at and what makes it stand out from its competitors, for instance, having a strong brand or unique technology. It's advisable to consider both the internal view of your strengths and the external view from customers and those in the same market.
- Weaknesses – Identify the things that hinder your best performance. These are your trucking business areas that require improvement, for example, poor customer service or poor location. Be realistic and consider both internal and external perspectives.
- Opportunities – This refers to the external factors that favor your trucking business. A keen look at your strengths and weaknesses could help point out

any untapped opportunities that could be brought out by changes in government regulations in your field or changes in technology.

- Threats – This refers to anything that could potentially harm your trucking business. This includes existing or potential competitors, changes in customer preferences, or new government regulations that could reduce your sales.

Conducting a SWOT analysis will enable your business to compete strategically within the market.

a) Regulations

You should know government regulations that can affect your trucking business—for example, changes in fuel prices or food safety rules.

Sales and Marketing

Strategizing how to gain the market share involves:

a) Marketing strategy

Take into consideration how you will promote and market your trucking business firm, or you could do the marketing on your own, for instance, having fliers printed and distributing them. Ensure that you have the costs you will spend on marketing and advertising and identify the media through which you will communicate. Some of these include local business magazines, posters, social media, etc. As you have all these, keep in mind your target regions and industries you're trying to reach.

b) Sales strategy

This is where you lay out plans on how you intend to sell your trucking services to potential customers with a view of generating revenue and, in turn, maximizing your profits. It involves identifying your target market and how you will appeal to them. You can employ the use of external sales agents or hire salespeople for your trucking company.

TYPES OF TRUCKING BUSINESS NAMES

Family Names

Choosing a family name for your trucking company can be a great way to build a business legacy. If you plan to start a family-run business and want to pass it on to the next generation, you will want to choose a family name. Some customers might also enjoy working with a company more focused on the family.

Location Names

If you plan to keep your trucking business within a specific geographical area, you may want to consider a name based on the particular location. This name will also appeal to customers who wish to hire local carriers. However, when choosing these names, also keep in mind any potential expansion plans since you don't want to limit yourself in the future.

Freight Type Names

If you are going to specialize in specific freight types such as reefer, hazmat, or other styles, you may want to consider a name with this type of freight in it.

Unique Names

In the competition, you may want to develop a unique name. Perhaps one based on culture or personality. The focus will be on choosing a name that is memorable to customers.

Mistakes to Avoid

There are three main mistakes to avoid. The first is to avoid choosing a name that is too common. The goal is to make customers remember you, and standard terms will confuse you. So prevent terms that are too similar to other businesses.

Second, you want to avoid choosing a name that is a cliche. Don't select words or expressions that aren't descriptive and focus on your business's unique aspect. Focus on positive stories and metaphors that describe your company, and you'll find plenty of options to choose from.

Lastly, while you want to involve family and friends in choosing a name, you also don't want to apply to too many people. This will give you too many options and can move you away from your business objectives. Instead, involve a few key people who know your goals and help provide you with severe and strategic opinions.

Set Up a Plan

Before you start working on starting your business, you'll need to have a plan in place and ask yourself a few critical questions. The questions will help you develop a plan for your business and aren't that difficult to answer if you already have a vision for your business.

Where Will You Base Your Business and How Far Will You Haul?

The base location for your business and the states you plan to haul freight before starting your business. If you choose to stay within your state, you may not need some licensing and costs associated with moving freight across state lines. For example, if you plan to haul across state lines, you'll need an MC number, and there are fewer requirements for transporting within your state.

Will You Do the Driving?

If you want to drive the truck at the start of your business endeavor, then you'll need more licensing. For a one-truck operation, you can save money on employee salary, but you'll still need to make sure you have your commercial driver's license, which does require some work.

Do You Plan to Hire or Contract Drivers?

While you don't have to set up operations in a specific way, you'll need to consider whether you plan to hire employees or work with contractors later on in your business. One of the more difficult tasks of growing your business is to find qualified drivers, and we'll discuss this in greater detail later.

Lastly, you need to ask yourself if you plan on specializing in a niche area. Let's consider why you should choose a niche for your trucking business.

Choose a Niche

Successful trucking business is to choose and support the right niche market. You purchase, the rate you charge, and the freight lanes you can service. As an owner-operator, you should focus on needs that are avoided by larger carriers. This will give you less competition, and you will still have many markets to focus on; let's consider some of the markets open to you and which one you should choose.

- Dry Van

With this option, you have flexible equipment, and you can use it to support several industries. It also presents a low barrier of entry since the equipment isn't costly. However, there is a lot of competition in this category. Many companies have many resources and new owner-operators like you who want an easy start to the trucking industry. With all this competition, it isn't easy to get a good-paying load and secure regular customers. So if possible, you do well to look in other areas.

- Specialized Loads

It is best to choose a niche industry that doesn't have as many competitors. Large carriers tend to avoid specialized loads since they are more complex. This means small fleets and owner-operators can have better success within the specialized load market. The type of specialized loads you focus on will depend on the permits, driving skills, and experience. Location may also be a factor within some industries. Consider the following niche markets that you can specialize in when starting your business.

- Fresh Refrigerated Loads ("Reefer")

This is an excellent option for a new owner-operator. Within this unit, the most comfortable industry to focus on is the meat and produce industries. There are many advantages to carrying these loads:

Fresh meat and produce are regularly transported, which means consistency.

Shippers are easy to find from the local markets to wholesalers.

Loads in this area are resistant to recession, so you have revenue stability.

The bottom line is these loads also pay well, primarily when you work directly with shippers.

- Tankers

Both dry bulk and liquid tanker loads are profitable. Liquid tankers offer two different options: food-grade liquids and hazardous materials. However, hauling these loads isn't easy and requires specific experience. There was also a higher cost of equipment when first getting started, especially for dry bulk equipment, which is very expensive.

- Flatbeds

This is another area where you can focus since most large carriers avoid these loads. The problematic issue is finding a profitable load for both going out and backhauling. However, you can also find other opportunities.

- Cattle and Livestock

Trucking businesses can also make a decent rate of hauling livestock. However, these rates will largely depend on your location. Livestock can be a good option for an owner-operator who is just starting and wants to stay local.

The steps in starting your business are ready to begin. You'll now need to develop a business plan.

When you want to start a trucking business, you must begin with an organized plan. Having a healthy business plan can provide your business with a roadmap to success, and you can quickly refine it as you grow your business. It will help you stay organized, identify, achieve goals, articulate your value to others, and prepare for potential obstacles.

However, it is worth the effort since you will need it when approaching lenders, investors, or partners to help start your business. A business plan will help you get the financing you need to start your business. The business plan will also provide you with a critical road map for all the steps you need to take when starting a trucking business.

A trucking company business plan will contain much of the same information as other business plans. According to the US Small Business Administration (S.B.A.), a healthy business plan is one of structuring, starting, running, and growing your business.

A trucking business plan will need to include industry-specific information. You'll need to display a knowledge of what you need to be both profitable and competitive. An excellent resource for this information is the Owner-Operator Independent Drivers Association (OOIDA). Before you start writing your business plan, you need to determine what potential backers need to know to meet your financial needs.

You'll also need to include some customized information specific to your individual business needs. Other than this, all business plans need to have the following:

- Executive Summary
- Company Description
- Services Offered
- Market Analysis
- Sale and Marketing Plan
- Funding Needs and Request
- Financial Projections

The details in each of these units will vary depending on whether you plan to be an independent owner-operator or a company owner operating a fleet of trucks. There may also be differences based on the type of freight you plan to haul and where you plan to work. In general, each unit needs to contain accurate and detailed information that allows investors or partners to know you've done your research on the industry and understand what is required to be successful.

What to Do Before Writing Your Business Plan

Before you write a business plan, it is good to do as much research as possible. This helps you write an effective business plan and ensures you are ready to get your business started as soon as you get financing. Before writing a business plan, it can be a good idea to have the following in order or prepared to start:

- Register Your Business
- Obtain an Employee ID Number (E.I.N.)
- Get a Federal D.O.T. Number
- Apply for an MC Number
- File a BOC-3 with the FMCSA
- Get the Necessary Insurance
- Set Up an International Registration Plan (IRP)
- Start an International Fuel Tax Agreement (IFTA) Account
- Get a Unified Carrier Registration (U.C.R.)

Information You Need for Your Business Plan

Before writing a business plan, you should educate yourself on the industry and the financial basics. You'll need to have a robust financial plan and a good understanding of permits to comply. You should know the following before writing a business plan:

- Determine operating assets compared to liabilities.
- Learn managing costs to project real financial success.
- Determine the cost of operations, both fixed and variable.
- Determine the level of cash flow needed to ensure success.
- Develop realistic procedures for operating based on freight you plan to haul and where you plan to travel.
- Research rates required by freight lanes and why they are different.
- Learn where you can get freight loads and when to use load boards.
- Learn about spot market versus contract rates.
- Know the advantages and disadvantages of axing a fuel surcharge to your pricing.

Whether you plan to handle the financial aspect of the business yourself or hire an accountant, accounting basics means you need to have a basic understanding of balance sheets, profit-loss statements, and how to calculate total assets and liabilities.

TIPS FOR BECOMING A SUCCESSFUL FREIGHT BROKER

What are the things that distinguish an average freight broker who manages to break even from a successful freight broker? Here's all the actionable wisdom you need to know about being an ace freight broker.

1. Keep A Varied and Broad Client Base.

That controls a massive chunk of your revenue moves its business somewhere else; you'll be in trouble. Therefore, even though you may have a few big customers bringing regular business, do not underestimate the power of building a broad client list.

2. Innovate

Another secret for acing the freight broker game is to be open to innovation and newer/more efficient ways of doing things. You can tap into other transportation-related enterprises to avoid stagnation. I know freight brokers who have diversified into consulting other freight startups, purchasing trucks, and becoming carriers. There's plenty of scope for diversification as a freight broker. You can be a one-stop-shop for all logistics services. Many trucking company entrepreneurs start as freight brokers. Keep innovating, adding new services to your business profile, and expand your market to grow the business. Learn the logistics and transportation business ropes as a freight broker and then transition into building a transportation company.

3. Get Rid of Defunct Carriers

Each trucking company has occasional service issues. However, if there are frequent lapses, you may have to take a call and drop the company from your database. If you are forever having issues with carriers, your clients will quickly move on to another freight broker or trucking company. Of course, initially, you can't tell if a runner is excellent or problematic. However, over some time, you'll know the difference between trucks that offer excellent and snag-ridden service. While you can overlook a one-off case of transportation snag, set some boundaries before it starts affecting your business on a broader scale. Remember, it is not the trucking company but your reputation as a broker at stake here. If you enlist too many defunct and problematic companies in your database, it'll put your credibility as a freight broker at stake.

4. Preserve Your Reputation

The freight broker business is all about networking and building relationships/connections. Focus on building an enviable reputation within the industry if you want to go a long way. Shortcuts or the easy way out if it's even remotely shady. Have the integrity to pass it even if it appears to be a huge opportunity. People notice these things. Plenty of people need reputed, dependable, and honest services. If you can offer it by keeping your vision firmly fixated on long-term goals, you'll increase your chances of acing the freight broker game.

Build your business on trust and integrity. Word can travel at the speed of a supersonic jet within the industry. Good or bad – companies will know what you are up to and make their business decisions based on your market reputation. One bad experience or one lousy practice leading to court loss can damage your business. There will be tough times and tough decisions to be made, but if you want to sustain long in the freight brokering industry, keep your integrity intact. Do it the right way. Avoid taking shortcuts or looking at quick gains and also focus on maintaining the highest service standards. This way, you will increase your chances of having happy pay for good carrier services and frequently associating with them.

5. Identify Your Niche

It is lovely that you've started a freight broker enterprise. However, what niche are you going to specialize in? This is an excellent way to be a large fish in a small pond rather than several other fishes are waiting for their profits share. Find an exact niche such as a dry van or frozen freight. Trucks and shippers operating in this niche will identify with your services, and you may end up getting a large chunk of profits in these niches. Specialized services will make your brand more sought after. If you are keeping your loads general, segment them effectively through various units on your website or search function.

6. Join A Professional Association

Being an active part of any industry needs connections. Join the Transportation Intermediaries Association, which is a trade organization created for third-party logistics service providers. You'll have plenty of professional contacts and networking opportunities. You'll also have access to education, top industry trends, and codes on the best practices to be followed within the industry. Becoming a part of a professional association has multiple benefits. You'll get to know many people from the industry and get business through referrals and word of mouth.

7. Never Stop Learning

Access to education is no longer a challenge, thanks to the internet. You can access online courses, free webinars, industry case studies, podcasts, YouTube videos, and virtually inexhaustible resources of information for upgrading your knowledge and skills within the freight brokering industry. These resources can help you stay within the industry loop at a marginal cost.

8. Keep in Mind The 80-20 Rule

The administrative duties involved in the business of freight brokering. This can be everything from making invoices to maintain a company roster to drafting emails. However, as an agent, you'll need to stay focused only on income-generating activities rather than spending a considerable chunk of your time on administrative tasks.

Use the 80/20 Pareto Principle, which states that 80 percent of our results come from 20 percent of the input. This means only 20 percent of your activities are accounting for 80 percent of your total marks. Use this principle to focus on those tasks that are producing those 80 percent results. Use this rule to identify that 20% of companies or clients contributing towards 80% of your output. It is common for 80% percent of a freight broker business' sales to originate from 20% of clients.

How can you use the 80-20 rule to maximize your profits?

First, identify the activities leading to 80 percent of your sales and invest more time in those activities. What are your main income-producing activities? What are the activities that boost your sales? In other words, you are identifying and channelizing those 80 percent of activities that are driving more revenue to your enterprise. Maybe, seeking referrals, cold calling, attending networking events, visiting companies is what is doing the trick for you. Once you identify these 20 percent activities, spend more time doing them. This is one of the critical secret approaches to growing your freight broker business.

Similarly, use this rule for customers. Identify your top 20 percent of clients. These will generally account for about 80 percent of your company's sales. Direct a significant share of your sales, promotional, and marketing efforts on similar customers. The truth is, not all business activities and customers contribute equally to the sales generated by your company. Some tasks are more challenging, others more straightforward. Some are more time consuming than others. Some have a higher value than others. Learn to identify functions that produce maximum value and increase them. The idea should be to get good returns on your investment, including time and other resources.

9. Avoid Rewriting the Rules or Reinventing the Wheel

While it is good to innovate and diversify, a system already in place doesn't reinvent the wheel. If you see most successful freight brokers applying a specific strategy, service, or marketing technique that seems to be working well, incorporate it into your business operations. You don't have to be unique and original all the time. Getting ideas that work from competitors, other freight brokers, logistics companies, and truck carriers can lead your business in the right direction. Do what's working for others, and scaling it up with your business sense.

At times, freight operators were looking to develop a brand new software system to learn catered to their needs. Don't waste time doing something different when people are getting results following an existing design.

10. Tone Down the Sales Mode

Don't talk as if you are selling something. Tone down your sales pitch and speak more conversationally, as if you are talking to family members and friends. Don't launch into sales mode as soon as you see your prospects.

Contrived/manipulated speech patterns, loud, exaggerated tones, slow and hypnotic sales inductions can get on the prospective client's nerves. Speak naturally and appropriately. Make it more conversational and relaxed so the prospect doesn't feel the pressure of doing business with you, which will make the prospect of associating with you less desirable. No one wants to talk to a robot who wants to sell. People like a show of humanity and compassion.

Also, always stay in touch with your contacts. I can't emphasize this point enough. Sometimes, freight brokers will stop communicating with companies or clients who refused their initial business proposal. Yes, they may have opted for another service over yours at the time. However, what's to say that they won't need your services in the future. For all you know, they may be having problems with their current service provider or may require additional carriers. Staying in contact with potential customers ensures that yours is the first name that flashes in their mind when they need last minute or emergency bookings. As a freight broker, you'll get plenty of last-minute businesses when shippers need carriers urgently. To bag these last-minute deals, you have to make an effort to stay on top of have refused business deals in the past.

Send out festival greetings, keep checking periodically, send them messages about new services or features you've added to the business and offer a promo code or discount on the first shipment. Ensure you are the first name that comes to mind for last-minute freight transportation deals.

11. Negotiations Over the Phone

Remember, as a freight broker, and you'll have to negotiate plenty of last-minute deals over the phone, which is very different from face-to-face negotiations. Don't let a customer catch you off guard. Prepare well in advance for the talks by clearly knowing your terms. What are the typical statements you will use to handle objections? What will you say to persuade your clients to agree to your words? To what extent will you negotiate? Carriers may pose questions about the freight shippers or your customers' wish to move, for which you must have answers ready.

Keep your voice polite, professional, and authoritative. Stammering or stumbling for words or appearing flummoxed at the client's questions doesn't help seal the negotiations in your favor.

LICENSING REQUIREMENTS FOR FREIGHT BROKERS

Due to fraudulent activities in the freight brokerage business, this industry is governed by strict regulations, and licensing requirements are part of them. A prospective broker cannot commence operations without the freight broker license, not even for an experienced broker to operate with an invalid license, which requires renewal. Before getting into the broker license requirements, I want to describe the steps involved in the process.

Procedure for Obtaining a Freight Broker License

The freight broker's license endorses the broker to operate. The government agency responsible for issuing freight broker licenses is the Federal Motor Carrier Safety Administration (FMCSA). Let us go through what a broker needs to do for them to obtain their permission. Before you can start planning on licensing your freight brokerage business, it is essential to formalize its existence by registering it in the state you wish to operate. Once registration and licensing are complete, your business can start running.

Legal Frameworks

As part of establishing your business, you need to choose the right legal framework to determine the structure. The differences in various business structures are in liability and framework. Together, let's go through the different business structures that are available.

Limited Liability Corporation (L.L.C.)

In this business framework, liability is passed to the business, not the business owner. This means the owner's personal property is protected should any mishaps arise while running the business. Profits and losses are passed to personal income through the business structure, bypassing payments of corporate taxes. Although corporate taxes are not paid, self-employment taxes are paid by business owners (Johnson, 2019).

Partnership

In a partnership business framework, two or more individuals bring together their financial, skillset, and information resources to accomplish their common business goal (Lancefield and Rao, 2010). Successful partnerships accumulate more profits with much less individual effort because there is shared input and combined skills. However, where people work in groups, conflicts are also inevitable.

Similar to an L.L.C., the profits and losses are passed to personal income. However, unlike an L.L.C., each partner is entirely responsible for the business's debt in a partnership. In an L.L.C., the partners are only responsible for the business entity's obligation only to the extent of their contribution (Esajian, 2020).

There are two types of partnership business structures, namely, limited partnership (L.P.) and limited liability partnership (L.L.P.)(SARS, 2019). In L.P.s, a general partner is responsible for making significant decisions and is liable for its debts. L.L.P. setups do not have general partners. All partners are equally involved and accountable for the company's debts (Pakroo, n.d.).

Sole Proprietorship

In this case, the business is solely owned by a single person, and separate business entities are non-existent. The company and personal assets and business and personal liabilities (SARS, 2019).

Corporation

Corporations are businesses owned by shareholders and are a good option if you intend to do away with the liabilities involved in partnerships and sole proprietorships. There are two types of corporations, Close (C) and Subchapter (S) corporations, suitable for a startup business differences between these two types of corporations are their elections of formation, tax reporting, governance, and shareholders' number (Pearson, n.d.).

The formation of an S corporation involves filing a 2553 form with the I.R.S., while the I.R.S. form does not need to be completed to start a C-corporation. Based on formation, not all states recognize C-corporations and S-corporations enjoy the benefit of not paying corporate taxes. Another difference is that C-corporations have a more relaxed way of governance. For instance, they are not mandated to hold annual corporate meetings, as is the case with S-corporations (Pearson, n.d.). Finally, S-corporations can have up to 100 shareholders, against the 30 to 35 shareholders allowed for the C-corporations, depending on the state.

OP-1 Form

The broker will file with the FMCSA, accompanied by a filing fee of $3oo. This form requests the broker to be given an MC number or a unique identifier for the company. This number is used by authorities to endorse compliance with regulations by the brokers. When there is a need to carry out audits and appraisals, the MC number is required. The OP-1 form contains the names and type of the company, as well as the type of operating authority, either "Broker of Household goods" and the "Broker of Property (except household goods)."

The application for an MC number can be made by mail or online. If online, the broker receives the unique identifier as soon as they apply. The application by mail route takes longer before the MC number is issued. After the FMCSA has issued the MC number, it is posted on the Register page, and within the next ten days, anyone can contest against the company (Lance, 2015).

Designate a Process Agent

In every state where a brokerage company operates and has offices, it is recommended by the FMCSA that the freight broker selects a process agent. This is the person who represents the broker in cases that requires legal intervention concerning allegations against the broker. The broker should identify the process agent that they wish to work with. A list of process agents is available on the FMCSA website, together with contact details. The broker should then contact the process agent, who will file Form BOC-3, which is for the designation of process agents, with the FMCSA.

Apply for Your Freight Broker License

With your MC number and surety bond (which we will go into below) handy, you may file your application with the FMCSA. The so plan. Once your application for the license has been approved, you can start business operations.

Surety Bonds

Of all the stages involved in applying for a freight broker license, securing a surety bond is usually the most difficult. This is mainly because most brokers are in the dark as far as surety bonds are concerned. A surety bond, also known as the BMC-84, is a requirement for freight brokers as first-time applicants or those up for renewal (Guineva, 2014). It is more of a credit line used to settle clients whenever work-performance shortfalls are evident on the freight broker's side (Guineva, 2014). They have been set as requirements to establish freight brokers' credibility by ensuring they pay carriers on time and ethically provide their services.

They understand these concepts:

- The Principal: the entity that will receive or applied for the bond. Essentially, the Principal is the freight broker.
- The Obligee: the party with the right to claim to the company that issues the bond if the Principal is at fault with the terms and conditions that the bond reinforces. This could be the carrier, for example, who may have a complaint on untimely payments by the freight broker.
- The Surety: the company issues the Principal's bond after the Principal would have paid a premium. The same company to which the Principal must reimburse if the Principal's customers would have filed any claims.

When the freight broker approaches a surety company, they must present their financial background, which is used to calculate their credit scores. The credit scores are essential for determining the premium that the brokers should be paid yearly, should the surety bond be granted. In most cases, the credit scores of new freight brokers, and experienced brokers who have had many claims on their bonds before, are low.

The maximum amount that the Surety pays for claims against the Principal's bond is $75,000 (Williamson, 2015). However, the Principal does not produce this money all at once. It is paid in the form of annual premiums. The payable premium is calculated as a percentage of the maximum expected amount, $75,000, which is anywhere from 1.25% and 10% inclusive. In monetary terms, this is between $938 and $7500. The premium percentage is studied every year, implying any improvements in the credit scores and experience affect lowering the payable premiums.

Once all the requirements are met, and payments are complete, you will be issued your surety bond, valid for one year from its issue date. The surety bond can be terminated by any of the involved parties, either the Principal or the Surety. Any notice should be sent to FMCSA 30 days before the cancellation of the surety bond. Please note, this application can be made online. Now that you have more of an understanding of what surety bonds are, considering why they are worth it.

For freight brokerage businesses that are just starting, there is usually less to no leverage for spending money on clients' settling claims because the cost is too high. Startup companies would not have attained financial stability yet, and all financial resources are channeled towards getting the business running. Therefore, a surety bond provides a feasible way to pay the claims without straining the business's early finances, considering that the money is produced in annual premiums.

The Surety does not just process any claim brought to their attention by the freight broker's clients. They investigate the request first, after which they then process the payments if the broker is found guilty. There are chances that the broker may be found not guilty, in which case the Surety legally represents the broker, and the broker is saved from losing money to the Obligee.

Just by having a surety bond, a freight broker is more trusted by shippers and carriers. They feel more secure working with the broker, as they believe that the broker must perform well by their surety bond's terms and conditions.

You might be wondering if there is another way to reinforce a freight broker's credibility, and there is with a trust fund. This is a way to offer broker security and payout claims leveled against them by obligees.

The Trust Fund

Also known as the BMC-85, the trust fund requires the broker to make a large payment upfront that they cannot touch. To better understand how this works, I will use an example adopted from business author Nye Longman who said, imagine the trust fund as a bank where you can only deposit. FMCSA has access to this bank and can use the money to settle any claims against you by your clients.

The trust fund does not work by depositing percentages of the total amount, as is the case with surety bonds. Instead, $75,000 is paid all at once and stays there as long as there are no claims made against you. Compared to a surety bond, the trust fund establishes your credibility in the eyes of your clients, or shippers and carriers because they will know you run an ethical business. Additionally, this ensures that in the case of anything unexpected happens, they are liable to compensation. This a more common option for established companies who can pay the large sum as well as the annual bank fee

OBTAIN LICENSES AND PERMITS FOR YOUR TRUCKING COMPANY

Trucking companies can be quite stressful to manage. This is mainly down to logistical challenges. Businesses must endure all sorts of risks, but the trucking industry is hazardous. Moving with loads across the states puts your truck under various risks such as theft, accident, natural disasters, and vehicle breakdown. Considering these risks, it is self-evident that you need protection regardless of whether you are an owner-operator or large-scale operator.

Choose Your Legal Entity

The issuance of permits and licenses dramatically depends on the legal entity of the business. For instance, a sole proprietorship's licensing demands are different from a limited partnership, a general partnership, an L.L.C., and a corporation. Various legal entities come with their benefits and shortfalls.

Some of the factors are affected by the legal entity you choose for your business. These include personal liability limitation, ease of transferability, new partners admission, investors' expectations, and taxes. When you assess all the legal entities' benefits and drawbacks, you might see that a limited liability company is the most suitable. It does not matter what your beginnings are; you may very well start humbly and advance your way to the top.

As an owner-operator, you will first have to receive special training and a commercial driving license before driving trucks. Also, your vehicle must have requisite certificates to operate.

These are some of the basic requirements that you may have to fulfill before starting and operating your own trucking company:

- Commercial Vehicle Operator's Registration
- Business Liability Insurance
- Assistant's Licenses
- Driver's Licenses
- Ownership Proof
- ID
- Fire Certificate
- Certificate of Incorporation
- Business Plan
- Business License
- Non-disclosure Agreement
- Employee's Handbook
- Employment Agreement
- Operating Agreement

Visit the United States Department of Transportation, the Federal Highway Administration, and the Federal Motor Carrier Safety Administration to check whether other legal requirements are required to set up your trucking business, especially if your niche is sensitive. For instance, moving hazardous loads might require additional certifications.

Insurance

You must take out various critical insurance cover before you are allowed to operate a trucking business. The trucking industry is precarious. It would be misguided to forgo insurance, considering that some of the risks can potentially ruin your business. Additionally, most clients want to work with trucking companies that have their insurance coverage in order.

These are some of the necessary insurance coverage needed for your trucking business:

- Physical Damage Coverage
- Commercial Auto Liability Insurance
- Bobtail Insurance
- Motor Truck Cargo Insurance
- Non-Owned Truck Insurance
- Occupational Accident Insurance
- General Insurance
- Liability Insurance
- Workers Compensation
- Health Insurance
- Medical Insurance
- Overhead Expense Disability Insurance

General Liability Insurance

This is an insurance policy that safeguards your business against some claims such as bodily injury and property damage that may occur during business operations. If you get a Business Owners Policy, some insurance companies will lump both General Liability Insurance and Property Insurance.

The General Insurance Cover safeguards your company against claims involving workplace accidents, unruly employees, and wrong delivery. Some insurance companies will require you to acquire a primary liability policy to be eligible for general liability.

Cargo Insurance

This is an insurance policy taken on the load being handled by a trucking company. This policy protects the business against loss or damage of the cargo from a road accident or fire accident. Additionally, it also covers unintentional clearance of freight, undelivered shipment, and late delivery. In this coverage, you decide your limits that inform what your insurance company would have to pay. You may have to choose your deductible limit, which is the cost incurred by a claimant. This policy covers the following vehicle types: tractors, cargo trucks, trailers, cement mixers, and dump trucks. This policy does not typically cover freight, including money, art, jewelry, tobacco, contraband, alcohol, and explosives.

Bodily Injury and Property Damage

The Bodily Injury policy covers injuries and accidents that might happen in transit. The procedure may be instrumental in facilitating, for example, the payment of medical bills. The Property Damage covers against property destroyed by road accidents. The policy allows you to set your limits.

Physical Damage Insurance

There are two types of physical damage insurance: comprehensive car insurance and collision insurance. The policies cover any damage done to trailers and trucks. The two approaches may be bought separately. Collision insurance covers collisions damage, while comprehensive car insurance covers damages from theft, fire, vandalism, and animal attack.

Excess Insurance

Sometimes, your company may find itself in circumstances that you had never thought of. This policy covers for the unexpected situations that your trucking company might find itself wedged in. This insurance policy has the potential to cover liability, running into millions of dollars.

Bobtail Insurance

This policy covers when your truck is not being utilized to transport goods, such as when your vehicle is repaired.

The Best Fuel Card Services

A fuel card – also known as the fleet card – is a card used for buying fuel at gas stations. Fuel cards may also be used to pay for expenses and maintenance.

Fuel cards offer a simple payment solution. It becomes easier to manage your fuel payments when you stop using traditional methods like cash and credit cards. Drivers do not have to move around with money to buy fuel, which enhances their safety.

Fuel cards reduce the amount of paperwork involved. Receipts accompany transactions that involve credit cards and cash. Over time, it can become quite stressful to track your expenses from stacks of receipts. Fuel cards streamline everything, and it becomes much easier to track your costs since payments are made from one account.

Fuel cards also give you more control. You ma-y specify what can and cannot be bought using fuel cards. Also, you may select the stations where the fuel card will be accepted. This goes a long way in easing fraud.

It is much cheaper to buy fuel using a fuel card because the pricing is consistent and wholesale. This allows you to budget your costs appropriately. Moving around with cash might affect you grossly in instances where the prices are unstable.

Most fuel cards offer rewards. It may be in the form of points to be redeemed in supermarkets or bonuses. This gives you a chance to save up while not constraining your budget before getting a fuel card.

Regional Limitations

Ask yourself where you will be using your fuel cards. Not all companies that offer this service may be operating within your area. Also, some companies may require you to limit your services to specific stations. So you have to perform due diligence to choose a company that suits you.

Control

Fuel cards may enable you to control the activities of your employees. Considering there are more services you can pay for with a fuel card, for example, pump and truck services, you may want to restrict them from paying fuel only.

Integrations

Some cards offer powerful integration tools geared towards collecting valuable data, which improves data analysis and making business decisions.

Fuel cards are just about the best way to cater to your truck or fleet's fuel expenses. Here are some of the best fuel cards:

Comdata

This fuel card has nationwide coverage. This card can be accepted in 600,000 stations since it can be used as a debit card. It allows drivers to pay for fuel, tolls, and other related expenses. The Comdata app enables users to manage funds, locate stations, and appraisal various stations' services.

EFS

This fuel card covers both the US and Canada. Some of its benefits include: (1) a 10 cent per gallon discount at all Flying J locations; (2) low fees for fuel transactions; (3) advances, (4) ATM withdrawals; (5) balance inquiry; and (6) money transfer. The card offers discounts on other significant items like tires, auto parts, equipment, and lubricant.

Fleet One

This card covers the entire country and extends its services to Puerto Rico and Canada. This card is accepted in about 90% of fueling stations in America. The card allows users to track the expenses by showing the balance on their online platform. The menu also provides discounts, reports on fuel activity, scheduling, and costs.

Fuelman

This card focuses entirely on commercial clients. Fuelman offers two types of fuel cards: Fuelman FleetCards and Universal Cards. The Fuelman FleetCards can be used in over 50,000 sites, and they offer discounts and alerts. The Universal Cards may be used anywhere MasterCard is accepted. The Fuelman app assists users to locate the nearest station offering their services.

Wex Cards

These cards are mainly used by government affiliates and are tailored to them, but anyone else can use them. The Wex Cards help you control your budget by keeping track of your expenses.

US Bank

The US bank fuel card is tailored for truckers. Users may process fuel transactions in various stations throughout the country, offering powerful data analysis tools.

Shell

The Shell fuel card may be used for transactions in all Shell stations. The user may be able to track their expenses.

BP

The BP fuel card is tailored for truckers. It is not only useful in facilitating fuel transactions but also reduces costs. There are various rewards and bonuses attached to the card.

ExxonMobil

ExxonMobil offers two cards. Both cards are entitled to a discount of 10 cents per gallon at ExxonMobil sites for the first six months and then 6 cents per gallon moving on.

Arco

The ARCO fuel card may be used at over 1,500 ARCO fuel stations across the country. The card features include password controls, online statements, vehicle, and mileage tracking, disabling stolen cards, and restricting the type of expenses.

Legal Requirements: Obtain A USDOT Number

If you are a freight broker involved in cross-border trade, you must apply for the Federal Transportation Security Administration (FMCSA). The FMCSA is a government regulatory agency that is part of the United States Department of Transportation. It supervises transnational trade and enforces security rules.

Since December 12, 2015, new brokers must file for authority via the Unified Registration System (URS). The URS is an online electronic registration system that will simplify the registration process for new applicants. Existing brokers with either an MC, USDOT, or FF number must re-apply for their broker authority on April 14, 2017, on-forth.

To apply, you must pay the $ 300 application processing fee. Once you provide your application, you will be assigned the USDOT number, which gives you the power to negotiate goods.

However, when completing the Consolidated Operator Registration, you will need to pay a continuous annual fee of $ 76/year.

Get a Surety Bond or Trust Bond

Each freight broker is responsible for having a guarantee or trust fund of $ 75,000. If you are using collateral, complete form BMC-84. If you are using a trust fund, complete form BMC-85

A surety bond or trust fund is proof of financial responsibility. This means that you have access to enough money (liquid assets) to meet your obligations as a business, and you can pay any potential claims. Because many people don't have $ 75,000 to post a bonus, they use an affiliated company's services. Surety companies will charge a non-refundable fee and ask the client to post a security asset like a house, car, equipment, etc.

The purpose of a secured bond is to ensure that a brokerage firm complies with all applicable laws and regulations and keeps its promises to your business.

Let's say you can never pay a claim: In this case, the affiliated company will pay the request and ask you to reimburse the affiliated company within 90 days.

Also, since surety bonds carry significant risk, the bond provider should verify your personal information, business plan, and credit history. If the insurance company evaluates your application and finds that everything looks good guarantee, but only a percentage. The insurance company from which you receive your bond will submit the required documents to the FMSCA.

Premiums for surety bonds can vary from 1.2% to 5%. The optimal way to reduce bond premiums is to have a good credit score. When you establish a name and credibility for yourself in the brokerage business, you will grow your trust with carriers and shippers, leading to better business outcomes.

For example, suppose ABC Freight Brokerage is located in Washington State, and it signs contracts with shippers and carriers in California and Oregon. Hence, the broker must designate process agents for California, Oregon, and Washington State.

You can designate yourself as the process agent.

How to Designate a Process Agent?

To designate a process agent, download and fill Form BOC-3. A freight broker can file on their behalf. Only one form should be submitted that covers all states in which your brokerage operates.

You cannot use a post office box as your address when filing form BOC-3.

Once you've completed the BOC-3 form, sign it, and send it to the following address:

FMCSA

1200 New Jersey Ave., S.E. (W63-105)

Washington, DC 20590.

Build strong industry relationships and partnerships

Business is just as much about people as it is about profits.

Even though you may be your company's owner, you are not expected to know everything under the sun, especially at the beginning. If you are completing each step, you will have a big chance to succeed at freight brokering. If you need to turn to a professional for information and assistance, you can speak with instructors and student advisors.

Other relationships you will need include attorneys, bankers, carriers, shippers, insurance agents, and accountants.

Carrier Relationships

Building a positive relationship with carriers is vital to operating your freight brokerage. Carriers want to work with brokerages that pay reasonable rates and pay on-time. As a freight broker, you want to provide the required information to the airline. For example, send the carrier information about your company, bank information, carrier references, and parts of your business plan, such as the mission statement.

Getting the first load delivered will likely be your biggest startup challenge. To make it easier to get your foot into the industry, you can network with carriers at local and national trade shows and conferences. Another way you can network with pages is by using a load matching service. For more information on load matching services. Remember; don't treat carriers as a means to an end, but rather as a critical partner for your business.

Shipper Relationships

A shipper is a party that has goods that need to be transported. In simple terms, shippers are your customers. Strong relations with shippers are essential if you intend to maintain a continuous flow of business. Most of your clients will be gained by cold-calling, referrals, networking, and contacts.

A neat way to get to know your shippers and their needs is to ask them their goals and their biggest challenges. Doing this will gain insightful information and provide a new service or product to meet your customer's needs.

A good broker communicates daily with ship his/her shippers to let them know their shipments' status.

Shippers deserve to know delays on their shipments, including mechanical breakdowns, severe weather conditions, and heavy traffic. The last thing you'll want is for the receiver to tell your customer that the load was not delivered on-time or was delivered damaged. Remember, your business reputation is at stake, and it is ultimately your responsibility to preserve your company's identity.

Banker Relationships

Stable relations with your banker are necessary for your freight brokerage. Quite often in this business, you will need to pay your carriers before the shippers pay you. If runners don't receive their payment on time, then they will refuse to work with you in the future.

Therefore, to solve this dilemma, you may need to bank on a credit line—lines of credit range from $200,000 to $300,000 for freight brokers. Instead of establishing a relationship with a banker that handles personal accounts, you will want to apply for a credit line from a commercial loan officer, preferably dealing with the transportation industry.

When applying for a line of credit for your freight brokerage business, you'll want to make sure your presentation is excellent. For instance, be sure to evaluate your business plan with the banker so that they can verify your business and finances.

Often when obtaining a loan, you need to lender something in collateral, such as truck equipment. Because you do not have assets you can put up as collateral, you will need to ensure your credit rating is good.

Building a relationship with more than one bank is also recommended. If a bank dissipates in a merger or acquisition, then you will be protected from any disturbances.

Attorney Relationships

Many freight agents wish to advance their careers to become a freight broker. You may be surprised to know that this situation can be a sticky one. It may seem practical for a freight agent to leave their employer and start their own business.

However, there are legal ramifications in this scenario. For instance, employee contracts such as non-compete and confidentiality agreements can prevent you from starting your freight enterprise. Hence, it is recommended you take your employee handbook and warrants to an experienced lawyer so that the attorney can evaluate the documents.

Scenarios like the one mentioned above are examples of why an attorney can be a valuable contact. Attorneys can be useful to freight brokers in many ways. Firstly, they can advise you of any potential litigation you or your business could face. Secondly, an attorney can help you collect bad debts. Moreover, an experienced business and transportation lawyer can assist you in establishing employee policies and procedures.

In any circumstance you do not know of the legal ramifications, you'll have your attorney by your side to guide you. Therefore, consider adding an attorney to your advisory board.

Accountant Relationships

An accountant is valuable to your freight brokerage every tax season. Accountants can help you develop your overall financial strategy. They can also contribute to organize financial data for your business and ensure you do not overpay any taxes.

Insurance Agent Relationships

A dedicated insurance agency that understands your business needs is invaluable. Establish a positive relationship with your insurance company. The right insurance agent can inform and consult the best policies and coverage you need as a freight broker. They can also help you create risk-reduction systems and can handle any claims on your behalf. Refer to step 8 for more information on freight brokerage insurance.

What to Do When the Unexpected Happens on The Road

Roadside Assistance

Many companies will provide roadside assistance to you as a truck driver. If you have purchased a new truck, often, it will come with a roadside assistance package.

Also, check your insurance policy. You may have lined items that include truck and trailer towing, rental reimbursement, and other coverage. Be sure to ask your insurance agent about this.

Breakdowns

First and foremost, do your best to steer your truck and trailer off the main road. If you can find a reliable shoulder, use it, but don't run your truck and trailer into soft dirt or sand. It will only cause more damage. If possible, try to get onto a runaway lane or other stable place and out of the way.

Investigate the problem. If you can fix something without further assistance, do so as quickly and carefully as possible. Before starting any repair, make sure to set out any required road triangles, flares, or other materials to signify a vehicle's danger off the road.

Make sure that any work you are doing does not place you in danger of oncoming traffic.

If the work required is beyond what you can fix, call for assistance. If you have a roadside assistance plan (which I highly recommend), contact them, and arrange the donation. Depending on your location, you may be waiting a while, so make yourself comfortable. Be sure to stay hydrated, especially if you have broken down in a remote location or one with hot temperatures.

Stay in your vehicle. You are safer in your car than sitting on the side of the road or examining your truck.

If this is causing a delay in your delivery, then arrange for a pickup from another driver or contact your client.

Accidents

Truck driving has consistently topped the list of some of the deadliest occupations in the United States, but it's not the inherent danger of the job; it's the accidents on the road. In 2015, over 761 truck drivers were killed on the road. Over the preceding five years, trucker fatalities rose steadily by 11 percent.

Experts have said that this increase has been due to rapid delivery from the rise of online shopping and next day delivery. Too often, drivers are urged- by companies or themselves- to go after the reward of finishing enough deliveries and lose sight of safety concerns.

Never leave the scene of an accident. If there is significant damage, call for a police officer to file a report for insurance.

Always check to ensure the freight has not been damaged, no matter how small or insignificant the accident is. Check all tie-downs and straps and see that it is secure.

If there is damage to the freight, immediately contact your insurance company. Also, get the client, explain the situation, and ask how they would like to proceed.

If you are injured, seek medical attention. Make sure you have your emergency contact information on you.

Damaged or Lost Loads

If your load becomes damaged or shifts, pull over immediately. Check for slippage of ropes, straps, or chains. If you are unable to fix the gear, call for assistance. Never drive a trailer where the freight is not correctly strapped into place.

Contact your client about the damage or issues. Be straightforward and honest but calm and concise. Inquire how the client would like to proceed. They may want the load returned to its point of origin or instruct you to continue the delivery.

If your load falls from the trailer and onto the roadway, stop immediately. Depending on the situation, you may require not only law enforcement assistance in cleaning up the freight, but you may be required to file a police report. Most likely, insurance companies will want the information for any potential investigations. Again, contact your client and apprise them of the situation.

What About the Freight?

You are bonded to deliver the freight to its destination. It is your responsibility; if your truck breaks down, you need to make arrangements to have your trailer picked up by someone and delivered to its destination.

If you can't call a friend, coworker, or fellow hots hotter who owes you a favor, then you might even have to get on the boards and hire someone else and take a hit.

If you have to leave the freight on the side of the road for any amount of time, make sure it is secure and tarped if possible.

Trailer Sway and Fishtails

Trailer sway can be set off by a large wind gust, icy roads, sudden braking, or even the passing of a large vehicle like an 18-wheeler. If you have incorrect tire pressure in your trailer tires, this can make a bad situation much worse.

Even before you start driving, there are things you can do to lower the possibility of swaying:

- Make sure your tires are properly inflated.
- Always be aware and driving defensively. Be ready for the unexpected.
- Use lower gears going uphill. On the way down, be gentle in using brakes.
- Consider anti-sway devices and hitches.
- Take potential sway-inducing situations such as icy roads, bridges, and wind gusts very carefully.

If sway happens, do not slam on your brakes, or you will begin to fishtail or possibly jackknife if you lose directional control. Reduce your speed gradually and apply the trailer brakes, which will help the situation.

As soon as possible, pull over to a safe place on the side of the road and examine the trailer to make sure it was the wind or an environmental issue and not because the trailer is damaged. It is also possible something may have come loose or have been injured in the incident.

Natural Disasters

You may never have to worry about this, but some drivers get caught in earthquakes, tornadoes, fires, and even riots.

The first rule is your life is more valuable than your truck. Even your client would agree that the part you were transporting can be replaced, while your life cannot.

So, if you find yourself in danger, abandon your truck and find safety. There may be times when you can safely lock up your truck and return, while other times will be a race for your life. We have all seen the horrible video of floods or earthquakes where drivers only have moments before their vehicle is washed away or crushed under a falling overpass.

Find safety and do not leave until you know it is safe or are told that it is. Contact your friends and family immediately to let them know you are safe. Then contact your insurance company and your client to update them on the situation. Again, your life and safety are of the utmost importance.

Theft

Prevention will ward off most average thieves. Make sure the cargo is secure and locked if possible. Make sure the doors are closed as well as any lockboxes.

For some reason, some people are against using tarps, but if you use them, they can be a great way to seal in cargo and lessen the temptation for people to mess with it. Looking under a well-strapped tarp is usually a bit more effort than most common thieves or criminals are willing to give.

If you do find that you have been robbed, contact the police and get a full report. Contact your insurance company. If the theft impacted your client's cargo, contact them, give them a brief assessment of the situation, and confirm that they want to continue the delivery or make other plans.

Your employment contracts are either as an independent contractor or through websites that will have clauses on theft liability. Consult them to know where you stand.

Armed Robbery

Armed robbery has always been a problem for truckers. When they are away from their cab getting fuel or even at a rest stop, they are tired, often a bit distracted, and not paying attention to their surroundings. This is when attacks are most likely to occur. The news is littered with stories of truck drivers being held up at gun or knifepoint for the money they have on them, their truck, or their freight.

Hijacking and cargo theft are real issues as well. According to federal statistics in 2016, over 600 trucks were stolen with over 700 trailers, a steady increase over preceding years. It's estimated that theft and robbery accounted for losses of over 170 million dollars in a year.

According to statistics, Los Angeles is the number one location for cargo theft with other high crime areas, including the New York metro area and the south, primarily Texas, Oklahoma, and Northern Louisiana.

There is a saying, "Cargo at rest in the trucking industry is cargo at risk." Always be aware of your surroundings and that of your rig and trailer. Park in well-lit areas, even if you are only going to be gone for a few minutes. Always be aware of your surroundings and who you are interacting with. Also, never allow someone else to handle or transport your cargo unless you know who they are. If you are highly concerned or in an area that has a high level of robbery or theft, consider a tracking device in your truck and trailer as well as an alarm and recovery system for your vehicle.

Health Issues or Emergencies

Make sure that your health insurance is valid in the areas you are traveling to. If your haul takes you across the border to a foreign country for some reason, make sure that your health insurance is valid there. You might need to purchase a temporary rider, which can be purchased online for a few dollars a day.

Keep open communication with people to know who you are dealing with and where you are traveling.

Fatigue

There was a time when truckers wore their exhaustion as a badge of honor. They would gather at the truck stop, swigging coffee and caffeine pills, and laugh about how long it had been since they slept.

Fast forward to today, public awareness, legislation, and a change in self-awareness has changed all of that.

You need to get enough rest, and if you are tired, pull over. Do not use supplements. Never falsify your logbook if you are working more than allowable hours.

You are risking your life and the lives of others: pullover and rest. No load is worth a crash.

DUI

Never consume alcohol before operating any vehicle; let alone your work vehicle. If you get pulled over, arrested, and charged with driving under the influence, you are in danger of not only losing your license, but your business, your truck, and possibly your freedom. If you have employees, you need to have the same policy with them. This is a serious matter.

If you or one of your employees is arrested for DUI- and this includes not only medical and recreational marijuana but over-the-counter drugs and painkillers as well, be sure to contact an attorney immediately. This is one of the most hurtful things that can happen to you as an owner-operator, and you are at risk of losing everything. Consult with your attorney about how to progress.

LOGISTICS

From the opening of the CBI theater through the end of 1943, there was a policy of no precise night flying, which was dependent on runway lights. Chabua, Misamari, and Mohanbari received marker lights and spare parts for generators and flight instruments in September. At Mohanbari on the 1st of November, the C-47s assigned moved to the western sector of the ICW, leaving only C-46s in place. Round-the-clock operations were started.

As with any other theater in World War II, there were always snags that affected the mission. More so than the other theaters, CBI was dependent on airlift for all mission supplies. Bad weather caused planes to be grounded or lost over the Hump, resulting in delays or tonnage delays. The loss of an aircraft over the Hump not only wasted the cargo and aircraft but possibly a crew as well. If it weren't the weather, the Japanese would shoot planes down or damage them on the ground during air raids. Any loss was a step backward for the war effort against the Japanese.

At China terminals, Japanese air attacks were a daily reality. More than one transport crew spent the evening under attack or waved off from a Japanese aircraft aloft field. If a plane was waved off, their choices of alternate bases were limited. Other commands may be under attack or were out of range because of reduced fuel quantities on board the aircraft.

Despite the weather, Mohanbari's tonnage in January 1945 was 7,718.184 tons completed in 1,793 trips. Mohanbari carried the most of any of the basses—19.2% of cargo had. Sookerating was second with 6,653.631 tons.

The receiving bases of the tonnage in China were:

- Yunnan—267 trips (2140 tons)
- Changi—49 trips (392.135 tons)
- Chengkung—56 trips (448.84 tons)
- Yangzhou—27 trips (217.35 tons)
- Luliang—72 trips (577.08 tons)
- Kunming—731 trips (5858.965 tons)
- Baoshan—258 trips (2067.87 tons)
- Tsuyung—95 trips (761.42 tons)
- Teaching—201 trips (1611.015 tons)
- Charting—34 trips (272.51 tons)
- Mangshih—3 trips (24.245 tons)

Safety Program

Under General Tunner's command, a Flying Safety Program was instituted. The seven points of the program were:

- Investigate the training of incoming pilots fully
- Check the weather as a means of combating existing conditions, i.e., icing, turbulence, computing wind velocity in good weather and bad

- Communications—use of radio compass, radio limitations, when and when not to use "May Day."
- Pilot Discipline and Airport Discipline— Checklists, pre-flight, and post-flight
- Briefing and debriefing—competency of the crew, thorough preparation of pilot for existing conditions en route. Debriefing—Competency, problem areas, corrections, and training needed, best weather reports
- Maintenance
- Airport Facilities—upkeep necessary to the safety

General Tunner felt that health checks should be made for each pilot before flying, and their diets regulated. "Eating gas-producing foods even hours before take-off would result in debilitating agony at high altitude." A crewmember not in good health could cause an accident just trying to get their points in for rotation home. One man could cause the loss of a plane and as many as 45-50 lives if the cargo were a group of soldiers. Pilots were monitored to ensure the safety of a flight. Each accident was to be thoroughly investigated. Maintenance procedures are done on the plane before flight, weather conditions, and the pilot's activities are scrutinized on and off duty. Pilot error was a primary cause of crashes, with the most susceptible: new, inexperienced pilots. Those over thirty with 2,000 hours or more of flying time were less sensitive. To this day, the first step taken when investigating any incident is to check the crew's training records, especially the pilot.

ATC Units

The lifeline established from Karachi (now part of Pakistan) to Dinjan (the CNAC base) and on to China was activated in early 1942 and served as the western ATC hub of the India-China Air Route. Airplanes, supplies, and personnel passed through the base from March 1942 until it was deactivated in late 1945.

Beginning in January 1945, passenger flights started. Scheduled Valley Flight 51, a C-47A with airline seats, left Chabua in the early morning and flew to Misamari. Flight 52 took off from Lalmanir Hat and arrived in Misamari in the late afternoon. A freight schedule for the Assam Wing operated on a similar program.

Cargos

Cargos fell into two categories—wet and dry. Wet cargoes included aviation gas; everything else dry, primarily munitions. A team of two enlisted men (usually blacks) served as supervisors, plus many locals loaded the planes. Indian Pioneer troops typically wore steel-cleated, oversized shoes, which were considered a fire hazard when loading high-octane gasoline drums. They were used on all dry cargo loads.

Aviation Gas

The main cargo hauled over the Hump was aviation gas in 55-gallon drums or on C-109s in leaky fuel tanks that had been installed. It was not unusual to see an elephant being used to load gas drums into a plane.

In 1945, gasoline and oil accounted for 60% of all net tonnage eastbound. Ordinance amounted to 15%. Seven 55-gallon drums were loaded forward of the center of gravity (CG), and seven drums loaded aft of CG. Another cargo was loaded between. The balance included placement of passengers and supplies for Air Corps technical, PX, and Quartermaster. Westbound aircraft had smaller loads; by 1945, they flew empty.

Vehicles

Vehicles, which were in short supply, had spare part issues as did the planes, and were not useable in monsoon weather from May to October. The unpaved roads were severely constructed and mostly consisted of mud due to the average rainfall of 200 inches/year.

When loading a jeep or larger vehicle into a C-46, it would be cut in half or disassembled, packed in the plane, and reassembled in China.

PX Supplies

At Chabua, the PX opened once every two months with restricted (severely limited) supplies of razor blades, soap, and toothpaste. In late 1943, candy bars, beer, cigarette lighters, and hair tonic became available. At Mohanbari, PX supplies were never abundant and hit still lower levels when toilet necessities were unattainable.

The word "limited" does not come close to describing the availability of everything needed, from clothing through the Quartermaster Corps, paper, office equipment, and Post Exchange (PX) items to food and tents. Proper attire for flight crews ranged from slow-to-be-delivered to non-existent. In December 1944, flight uniforms arrived. Before December 1944, the aircrews would wear whatever they could find. In the winter, they would wear two or three layers of clothing—even blankets.

Equipment sent from bases already in operation to others for the start-up was slowly replaced, if at all. If the equipment was returned, it was generally worn beyond use. Oxygen, necessary to fly at the altitudes to clear the lower spine of the Himalayas, was not available. O2 masks were in very short supply. Oxygen had to be passed to the Assam bases from Calcutta. An oxygen generator plant was built later on in operations at Chabua. The plant exploded on more than one occasion, causing flights to be grounded or made without oxygen on board.

Requisitions

Capt. C. F. McLaren, Jr, Wing Supply Officer, reported in an interview that many requisitions from China were missing, causing a shortage of supplies in China. The Air Corp Supply attempted to trace back requisitions and expedite the flow of the stores to China. Many of the petitions were never received by the Depot at Chabua. During the investigation, no evidence was found to explain how the requisitions had been lost. The use was for China to send a petition to the Depot at Chabua, sending Calcutta's petition (Dum Dum). It was decided to cut out the middle man and send the requisitions straight to Dum Dum. This change was successfully implemented between March and April 1945. Removing the middle man at Chabua eliminated missing requisitions.

Cargoes Out Of China

Traffic out of China included troop transportation for combat training in India. Strategic materials such as were considered essential to the war effort:

- Wolframite ore, a form of tungsten
- Tin
- Hog bristles
- Mercury
- Silk

Part of the reason the listed items were deemed strategic was to keep them away from the advancing Japanese. Wolframite was refined in China and sacked, like flour, in five-pound bags. Tungsten was used in the U.S. to make armor-plate steel.

HOW TO NEGOTIATE YOUR WAY TO A THRIVING BUSINESS?

Negotiation is a crucial part of the freight brokerage business. Learning how to go about negotiating with your clients, shippers, and carriers are one of the ways you can ensure your business grows.

We will talk about the importance of negotiation in the freight brokerage business. We will also look at tips that will help you become a good negotiator and some of the common mistakes people make during negotiations that can make them lose their businesses.

It builds respect: Respect is an essential aspect of any business. It becomes challenging for you to build lasting relationships with your clients, carriers, and shippers without regard. It's also crucial for your team, as this is key for improving their productivity. Your negotiation skills can either make or break the respect your team, clients, shippers, and carriers have for you.

The impression you leave people with after a negotiation leaves a lasting impression that can impact your business, future talks, and reputation in the freight broker industry. When it comes to negotiations, you want to be firm and confident, and you don't want to come across as a pushover.

This will help build respect and maintain relationships with your shippers, clients, employees, and carriers.

You create win-win situations: Contrary to popular belief, negotiations are not about winning over other parties; they are about coming to an amicable solution for all parties. There is genuinely no point in negotiating if your primary intention is to ensure you come out on top. Win-win negotiations explore both positions and come up with mutually acceptable outcomes that offer both parties what they want.

Negotiations in the freight industry can quite often create win-win situations for all parties if handled correctly. So, how can you make a win-win situation for your business and other parties during negotiations?

First, separate the people involved in the negotiations from the problem. Avoiding identifying negotiating parties with the problem helps you ignore your differences and focus on the real issue at hand.

It helps you see things from your opponents' perspective and arrive at a fair, reasonable, and beneficial deal for both parties. Secondly, focus on the interests of both parties and not the positions. Once you choose to focus on the interests of all parties involved in the negotiations and not the works, it becomes relatively easy for all parties to come up with a solution despite the company's position.

The best negotiators in any business are the people who create win-win situations for all the parties involved in the negotiations.

Build relationships: The negotiation process is one method you can use to build relationships with stakeholders in your company. An excellent negotiator understands that negotiations are not only done in closed rooms. They are also done outside the negotiating room. They build a relationship with the negotiating party before negotiations start to enable you to build relationships and maintain them.

Tips to Help You Become an Excellent Negotiator

Listen: An exceptional negotiator knows how to keep quiet and listen to the other side when talking. They are like detectives probing the other negotiating party with questions and then keeping quiet to listen to their response. In business, listening can solve so many quarrels. The more you listen, the easier it becomes for you to determine what the other party requires from you.

Do your homework: Before entering a negotiating room, do your homework. It helps when you come fully prepared to discuss a particular issue once you learn more about it. You can identify the options you have, what the other party's needs are, and what pressures both parties have experienced concerning the issue at hand.

You are doing your homework before negotiations increase the chances of success. You also make accurate decisions based on what you found out about the other party. You can also develop a win-win situation for both parties much easier if you do your research in advance. More often than not, coming up with a winning solution comes down to how prepared you are before the negotiation even starts.

Characteristics of a Successful Freight Broker

Success is not defined by the amount of profit your business makes or the amount of money you have in a bank account, but by the positive impact, you cause in your surroundings.

We will talk about the characteristics of a successful freight broker. This will help you prepare the grounds for yourself as you start your freight brokerage business.

1. Trustworthiness and honesty

I cannot stop stating how important trust and honesty are in the business world. Without these two factors from the very beginning of your business, it becomes tough for you to maintain relationships, let alone create them. A freight broker that is honest and trustworthy always attains results even when the odds are against him/her. The clients trust that you will consistently deliver even when there are challenges along the way.

Being honest ensures that you are also transparent when you are communicating with shippers and carriers. The more transparent you become, the easier it is for you to build trust with everyone around you.

Trustworthiness comes as a result of being honest. When you are honest about freight conditions or what you can and cannot do as a freight broker, it makes it easy for you not to make your clients empty promises. Consequently, freight brokerage businesses that only think of themselves have more to lose than companies honest with their clients from the very start.

2. Resilience

We all know that no business in the world is devoid of challenges and failures. Any successful freight broker can tell you that they once felt like giving up because of their difficulties while in the freight brokerage business. However, what sets them apart from other freight brokerage businesses that gave up shortly after starting is the resilience they had.

Resilience is your ability to bounce back and adapt even in the face of unexpected challenges. It is the ability to know when not to give up or give in to your business's problems.

What makes resilience an essential characteristic for freight brokers to have?

- Resilience helps you develop mechanisms, which you can use for protection against overwhelming experiences in business.

- It helps you learn how to create a balance in your life during those stressful and challenging moments as you run your business.
- It keeps you from developing mental health issues such as anxiety due to the problems you face.

Challenges do not easily rattle successful freight brokers; they can keep calm, make decisions, develop possible solutions, and make their customers happy even when the odds are against them.

3. Flexibility

Flexibility is another significant characteristic almost every freight broker should learn to develop. Flexibility is vital as it enables you to make decisions even when you are up against a wall concerning a particular order.

You can shift things around on behalf of your clients, rearrange your loads, and make your clients happy with the decisions you make on their behalf.

Flexibility makes it easy for freight brokers to deliver quality, even when faced with tough challenges. It makes them not succumb to the chaos and focus on the goals they have for their business.

4. Self-motivation

Successful freight brokers are driven by a passion for ensuring that their businesses grow despite the challenges they face.

They have a reason to keep pushing on even when the job becomes quite monotonous.

This is what we call self-motivation. Whether it's perfection, time, money, family, or acquiring enough finances to start a particular project, whatever the reason, they can wake up early in the morning and get going. The reason for their motivation is what gets them through the entire day.

Surprisingly, the motivation that successful freight brokers have is not always driven by the amount of money they make; sometimes, it is purely an inner drive that makes them want to see the job done in the right way using the appropriate methods. They are efficient at what they do, enabling them to build relationships with customers, shippers, and carriers.

Even when their businesses are slow and not generating plenty of profit, you will still find them ready to get to work. Business people who have no self-motivation often struggle to keep their businesses afloat due to the lack of passion and pride needed to succeed. This makes it easy for them to throw in the towel when faced with challenges.

5. Customer-oriented

A successful freight broker understands that his/her business cannot run if his/her customers are unhappy. Therefore, a successful broker will make his/her business customer-centered.

After all, a satisfied and happy customer will always be loyal. Successful freight brokers understand their customers' value in their business, and they make it their mission to satisfy their every requirement.

They are devoted to their customers' interests, making it possible for them to grow their business. This case involves the shipper's part to see their freight safely delivered and done on time.

A deep sense of customer focus makes it easy for freight brokers to earn referrals bringing in other customers without having to go out looking for them. The more your business focuses on its clients, the easier it becomes to build and maintain a long-term relationship with all your clients.

Therefore, if your company is not customer-oriented, then try to incorporate methods that help you put your customers first and allow them to express their interests in your services.

DIFFERENT MODE OF SHIPPING

Transport by Oceans – Sea Freight

Sea freight is the transportation of goods and equipment from one place to another by sea. It's also known as ocean freight. It's the method of transporting goods, containers, and other materials by cargo ships from the goods' origin to the goods' destination.

Sea freight is one of the oldest means of transport since ancient times, and man has used the seas to move goods for short distances. With the global market place and the economies of cheaper production in countries like China and India, it becomes more economical and less expensive to produce labor-intensive products in such countries and ship them worldwide to the consumers.

It means of transportation in today's age. Entire industries have developed to support the massive ocean-going ships carrying cargo. This growth has been brought about by standardization and containerization.

Goods were usually shipped as breakbulk cargo, where they were typically piled on the ship. This resulted in significant problems like underutilization of space, loading and unloading problems, unstandardized loads, expensive to ship, etc.

The modern steel container has come into use and is designed as a standard container size, accepted and adopted by all the world's shipping lines and carriers. The ships are purpose-designed with these standard containers and dimensions in mind. Not just the boats but the transport trucks, the container terminals, the rails, etc., have all been designed to accommodate this standard container size to allow it to be transported anywhere in the world.

The invention of a container with standardized sizes and dimensions in the middle of the 20th century by businessman Malcolm Mclean revolutionized the ocean shipping industry.

There is an extensive history behind how the container came about in its current state, beyond this book's scope.

There are major shipping lines and carriers that specialize in the transportation of containers. The biggest of them are Maersk, CMA- CGM, Mediterranean Shipping Company. ETC.

Sea freight keeps feeding the world's demands and needs for internationally produced goods available locally.

Transport by Air – Air Freight

Ever since the first flight in the year 1903 by the Wright brothers, people and companies have been looking for ways to utilize aircraft for moving cargo. The first air freight occurred in the year 1910 when a department store moved a bolt of cloth. Airfreight started slowly but surely developing around the world, transporting goods. The first regularly transported items by airfreight were mail and parcels.

Airfreight started with passenger aircraft. Some of the space on the flights were utilized for cargo. It was only later that dedicated aircraft know as freighters, were developed to transport cargo only. Airlines found it most profitable to transport passengers on the main deck and load them in the aircraft's belly. Airlines found it very lucrative and profitable. It's estimated that more than 50% of the airfreight moves in this manner.

Airfreight was slower to develop as expected and was a small part of the freight industry.

Airfreight has quite a set of complicated rules and requirements, but we focus on sea freight beyond this book's scope.

Any cargo moved from one place to another by a charter, commercial, or passenger aircraft is considered air freight. It can be one of the quickest modes of transport, but also one of the most expensive. Airfreight charges are usually on a per kilo basis and depend on the cargo's dimensions and volumes. Cargo can also be transported to remote locations by this mode of transport.

Using air freight and other modes of transport like road and rail can result in one of the largest shipping networks. It is one of the fastest and most reliable methods of transportation.

There are a few options with airfreight:

- Next Flight out or Expedited cargo

Under this option, cargo is shipped out on the first available flight, which is the most expensive option under air freight.

- Consolidated Shipment

Airfreight carriers and providers have flights moving on a set schedule. They accept and consolidate cargo from different shippers and load it together. This allows them to have planned programs. This allows the carriers to sell the freight at a cheaper rate to the shippers. But they will usually wait until they have a set amount of cargo before they ship, which can sometimes lead to delays.

- Deferred cargo

Under this option, the airline loads the cargo on lower propriety once they don't have any other higher-paying shippers and there is space available. This kind of airfreight often the cheapest and offers maximum savings. However, cargo can be delayed for many days.

- Chartered Flights

Air Chartered flights are dedicated flights for transportation based on the requirements of the shipper. The shipper gets exclusive access to the plane to move whatever cargo he may want. This is one of the most expensive options for air freight.

Transport by Road – Road Freight

Road transportation, or sometimes referred to as road haulage, is the transportation of goods from one place to another by road. This could be either national or international. National road freight is when cargo is moved by road within the boundaries of a country. This could be on trucks, pickups, vehicles, etc. International shipment is when the load is carried on trucks from one country to another by road.

Road transportation is one of the most efficient modes of transport when moving cargo overland. It's significant for landlocked countries where there is no access to oceans for sea transport. Zambia, Zimbabwe are some of the landlocked countries and depend on road transport for their trade needs.

Even if cities are based near the port, road transport would be used to move cargo to and from the factories to the port area for further transportation to other places and countries. Thus, road transportation will be an integral part of your logistics and supply chain even though you would be near the port. Even when the cargo is moving by air freight, the shipment would likely be transferred by road to the airport.

Road haulage can also be one of the significant modes of transport for large masses of land, countries like Australia, which is quite large depend on road transport for their shipping needs. Thus, road transportation could be one of the most important modes of transport.

One of the benefits of road transport is that it can work on a door to door basis. Cargo can be collected from the shipper's location and delivered right to the entrance of the consignee. The road transportation industry has higher rates of accidents, dependence on traffic conditions, and fluctuating cost due to fluctuation in fuel costs. There could be other delays due to permits and road rules regarding the number of driving hours etc.

Demand for road freight transport services can be a leading indicator of a country's economic growth, and it serves as one of the main links in the supply chain.

Parcel and Mail Service

Delivery of parcels and mail service has been in existence since ancient times. Use of animals for transport was widespread, from camels to horses to pigeons, all sort of animals was used. In Alaska, dog sleds were abused, while in Australia, camels were used. The invention of the wheel gave way to stagecoaches and animal-drawn carriages. But with the design of the motor, parcel, and mail delivery were radically changed.

Parcels and couriers are usually limited to small packages of documents. The cost of the properties is generally based on per kg. Some of the most significant parcel/courier companies globally are UPS, DHL, TNT, etc.

Today companies like Amazon have taken package delivery to the next level, from express to the same deliveries, setting the industry standard and raising the customers' expectations.

Transport by Rail – Rail Freight

Rail freight is the use of railroads for moving containers and cargo by trains. This is usually done by freight trains or trains with a combination of passenger cabins and freight cars.

A Freight train or goods train is a train with freight cars hauled by an automotive engine on a railway track. These freight carts have provisions for loading containers, loose cargo, or even break-bulk cargo. Freight trains are usually specialized trains with purpose-built cars designed to carry loads from one place to another. It usually acts as an intermodal mode of transport and quickly and efficiently reaches the inner regions.

The rules and regulations governing rail freight differ from country to country.

Rail freight can be one of the more efficient modes of transport when measured in terms of energy spent on moving a shipment, and it can be one of the more efficient means of transportation. It can be incredibly cost-effective when moving bulk cargo like coal, iron ore, etc. when transported over long distances. Rail freight usually connects remote locations where regular service is needed, like mines or processing facilities located far away from major cities.

However, rail freight can require heavy investments for setup and maintenance since the cost of laying down railway lines, engines, etc., can be quite expensive. It can also lack flexibility compared to the road since once the railway tracks are laid down, there need heavy investments to expand the rail network.

Rail freight uses many types of goods wagons and freight cars; some of these are

- flat cars for heavy or bulky cargo

- boxed or covered cars for general cargo

- refrigerated vehicle for shipment, which is perishable.

- Tankers for liquids and gases

- Low loader cars for vehicles

- Open top wagons for bulk material

Each kind of wagon has its advantages concerning cargo handling.

One of the significant disadvantages of rail freight is its inflexibility compared to road transport. It requires heavy investments and a thorough analysis of demand before new rail lines can be developed. The cost is relatively high.

PICKUPS FOR AIR IMPORT FREIGHT

The actual pickup from a Container Freight Station (CFS as the industry refers to them) or location that would be shipping imported cargo is a bit of a challenge if the paperwork is not done correctly by both the Freight Forwarder and the Carrier. This transaction is where 90% of the breakdowns in the movement of the cargo will occur.

We all have tried this game one time in our life, the whisper game where you have ten people in a circle and whisper one a sentence and have them whisper to the person next to them the same sentence. The punishment will differ from how the first person stated it.

If a Freight Forwarder contacts a Carrier for their services, you now have one additional hand in the communication process. In some cases, depending on the chain of custody, you could have more than one different hand in the process. With Air Imports, you could have the Freight Forwarder (A) provide the Customs clearance to allow the freight clearance to ship, but they in return, by the way, it is sold have to turn it to Freight Forwarder (B) and then the terms require them of how it is sold to arrange the trucking. This happens a fair bit in the Freight Forwarding process.

We will explain the actual process and give some tips on avoiding some of the communication challenges.

Essential Tips for Recovering Freight:

- Ensure you have a Delivery Order (with all your information noted earlier; most locations will require a driver to have this in their hand when they arrive for the pickup).
- Ask if this is cleared for recovery from all government agencies (Example – US Customs cleared).
- Check to see if all charges are paid to the location you will be picking up the cargo from (they usually have a fee they charge for handling).
- See if they need wooden skids at pickup (when the economy changed, some locations require a skid exchange at pickup).
- Find out the ready time (just because the cargo arrives at 8 am does not mean you can pick up the shipment at 8 am; depending on if the load is trucked or flown directly into the pickup location, they require from 2-6 hours after the arrival time for pickup. So, in this example, if cargo arrives at 8 am and is flown into the location of pickup, your load could not be ready for pickup until 2 pm that day, depending on the city you are in).

Check on the hours of operation at the pickup location.

- Verify what the cargo's LAST FREE DAY (LFD) to pick up is (most locations give three days free, and they charge a large fee afterward, that the Forwarders try to avoid paying. In some cases, the trucker could be responsible for paying this fee if they fail to recover the freight from the location on this date.

- Find out the delivery requirements once picked up. Some of these locations have significant delays in recovering, so you may not be able to meet the delivery requirements (if this ever happens, it's always best to inform the Freight Forwarder of any delays. In most cases, they can work around the delay, but they have to know it is happening).

Even though we live in an electronic environment, we have found the most efficient way to communicate, which is a simple phone call; colossal issues can be reduced to a simple phone call. Trust me when I say this; if ever in doubt, pick up the phone and need to confirm the question you may have.

Deliveries for Air Export Freight:

The traditional trucking process is applied the same way in the Freight Forward industry, and the truck will deliver the product. Once empty, it will begin its pickup process to fill the car to return to maximize the load capabilities.

You have one of 3 processes that will happen for Air Export cargo. It will be pick up by the Local P&D, LTL, or expedite carrier depending on the shipping requirements and flight requirements to export out of the United States.

There are additional guidelines that watch over the industry that TSA has in place, and we will not elaborate on these items due to security requirements. However, know they do exist to regulate security in Air exports.

We will walk through the following points to assume that the TSA guidelines are in place and being followed.

Most Carriers will begin their pickups in the area they are around lunchtime or there beyond, depending on the nature of the carrier's location, either bringing the cargo back to the Freight Forwarders warehouse's location (independently or company site) or to the airline directly. In most cases, the LTL Carrier does not deliver the cargo directly to the airlines, some Expedite Carriers will, and in some cases, the Local P&D Carrier will.

The shipment can be delivered earlier than the flight date, but most airlines have limited space and multiple flights, so it's challenging for the cargo to be delivered very prematurely. If a shipper sends something via plane, they pay much more money to have this shipped as they are not shipping to have it sit. They want it moving.

CONCLUSION

The trucking, Freight, airfreight, logistics, and transportation companies in the world all have a common goal: to transport things from one place to another. Some companies specialize in ocean shipping, where the goods are transported by boat. Others specialize in trucking, where goods are transported by truck. Even a few specialize in airfreight where goods are transported via plane. Recent advancements in technology have brought about changes within these industries that have revolutionized and improved all aspects of trucking. One such promotion comes from the introduction of GPS tracking devices for trucks. Such devices provide greater security for drivers and trucks, help protect cargo from theft, and help keep costly accidents at bay.

GPS tracking devices for trucks not only help ensure greater security for the truck, driver, and cargo, but they also help to reduce costs associated with damage. Uninsured drivers who cause accidents often become a significant financial burden to trucking companies and negatively affect a company's bottom line. Insurance companies can quickly determine if liability is on the driver's part or someone else's part with GPS tracking systems. This saves time and money spent fighting over this responsibility. When an accident does occur, knowing what direction a vehicle is moving can help determine what caused the accident. If a driver from another company caused an accident, it would be possible for insurance to be denied entirely depending on negligence versus intent. Deprived of these systems in place, it would be impossible to distinguish between these factors. A monitoring system also allows companies to verify if their drivers are driving according to established guidelines, thus keeping costs low when drivers are not using their trucks properly.

GPS tracking systems have also helped protect cargo by increasing security around vehicles from theft or damage by thieves looking for valuable items inside trucks. Even when not equipped with GPS, any item of value on a car is often worth more than the truck itself. This is owing to the relatively low cost of trucks than their cargo and the ease in which they can be stolen. The American Trucking Associations (ATA), an organization representing most of the trucking companies in the United States, estimates that about 7,500 trucks are stolen every year from the United States alone. If a truck runs out of fuel or breaks down, it can become an easy target for thieves because drivers often leave their trucks unattended while they seek help. The use of these systems makes it possible to track a truck's location at all times and thus allows companies to follow these stolen vehicles in real-time.

One negative aspect of GPS tracking systems found in many trucking companies is that some drivers feel like they are carrying a burden when using this technology. They feel as though this technology takes away from their independence and gives them more responsibility instead. They also think that these systems are being used by management as tools for monitoring drivers. This decreases their emphasis on providing individualized attention to drivers, leading to reduced driver satisfaction levels.

CPSIA information can be obtained
at www.ICGtesting.com
Printed in the USA
BVHW041156090321
602109BV00016B/324